Coral Reefs

Written by Moira Butterfield

Contents

Collins

Stanley Primary School

All about coral reefs

Amazing ecosystems

A coral reef is a big underwater structure made of a stony substance called calcium carbonate – also called limestone. It's made by millions of tiny creatures called stony or hard corals. Living corals, marine plants and animals all live on top of the reef structure.

A coral reef is an **ecosystem** where there's lots of natural life. Although coral reefs cover less than 1% of the ocean floor, they're home to around 25% of the world's marine animals and plants.

Coral reefs are spectacular-looking ecosystems rather like undersea gardens.

Where to find reefs

Coral reefs grow mainly in shallow warm water, so most of them are found in the warm oceans of the tropics, the area of the world on either side of the **equator**.

Conditions have to be just right for corals to grow. Most of them need plenty of sunlight, which is why the seawater around them must be shallow and clear. It must be roughly the temperature of a lukewarm bath, with just the right amount of saltiness.

A few rare corals grow in deep cold water.

Record-breaking reefs

The biggest reef on the planet is the Great Barrier Reef off the northeast coast of Australia. It's the world's largest structure made by living creatures.

The world's longest reefs

1. **Great Barrier Reef**
   Length: 2,300 kilometres
   Location: in the Coral Sea near Australia
2. **Red Sea Coral Reef**
   Length: 1,900 kilometres
   Location: in the Red Sea near Israel, Egypt and Djibouti
3. **New Caledonia Barrier Reef**
   Length: 1,500 kilometres
   Location: in the Pacific Ocean near the island of New Caledonia

The Great Barrier Reef is the biggest coral reef in the world.

4

How old are reefs?

Most of today's coral reefs have taken between 5,000 and 10,000 years to grow.

Round boulder-shaped corals only grow by around five to 25 millimetres a year. Smaller branched corals can grow by as much as 20 centimetres a year.

Black coral, which is not always black, as you can see!

The oldest living coral ever found was a species called black coral, growing off the coast of Hawaii. Tests showed it to be 4,265 years old! It grew between four to 35 micrometres a year (a human hair measures around 80 micrometres across).

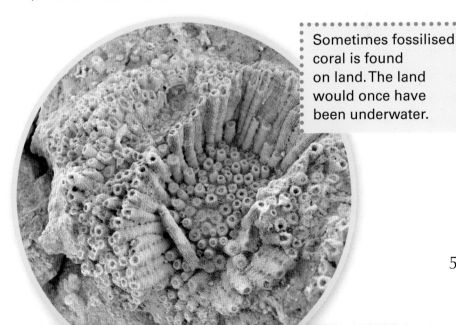

Sometimes fossilised coral is found on land. The land would once have been underwater.

How a reef is built

Tiny baby corals called **planula** float in the ocean. They settle on underwater rocks near land and grow into soft mini coral bodies called polyps. The polyps of the stony coral family protect themselves by making a hard limestone cup-shaped skeleton around their base. They produce the limestone in their bodies using material they absorb from the sea around them.

When a polyp dies, it leaves its little stone skeleton behind and new corals grow on top. Eventually enough polyps grow and die off for the limestone to build up into a reef.

All about polyps

A stony coral polyp has a body that looks like a little bag. There's an opening for a mouth, with tentacles around it. Coral polyps are usually nocturnal, which means they hide in their skeletons during the day and extend their tentacles out to feed at night.

Stony coral polyps are very small – only around one to three millimetres wide. They live together in colonies. Imagine how many billions of polyps it took to build the Great Barrier Reef!

coral polyps opening at night

tentacles

limestone cup

a coral polyp

coral reef

7

Coral reef shapes

Coral reefs grow in different shapes. There are three main types – fringing, barrier and atoll. Fringing reefs grow close to the shore. There may be a very shallow, narrow strip of water between the reef and the shore. Fringing reefs are the most common kind of reef around the world.

a fringing reef along the coast of Whitsunday Island

Barrier reefs also grow around coastlines, but they have a deeper, wider area of water called a lagoon between the reef and the shore.

Atolls are rings of coral in the middle of the sea, with a lagoon in the centre. They form when an island, surrounded by a fringing reef, sinks or gets flooded by the sea, leaving the reef behind. Often the island will be the top of a sea volcano. Atolls are most common in the South Pacific and the Indian Ocean.

At this section of the Great Barrier Reef off Queensland, there's a lagoon between the reef and the shore.

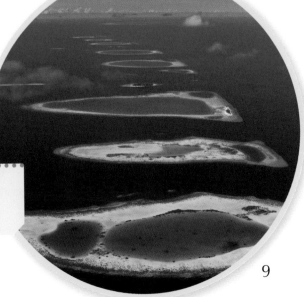

a group of atolls, coral reef rings with seawater in the centre

9

A coral's food

Stony corals have secret helpers that they rely on to survive. These are the zooxanthellae, which are tiny **algae** that live inside the bodies of the polyps. The algae **photosynthesise**, which means they use sunlight to make sugars. The coral polyps use the sugars as food, to grow and stay healthy.

Without the algae, the stony coral would eventually die. Without sunlight, the algae would die. That's why stony corals grow in shallow seas where they can get lots of light.

The slit in the middle of this plate coral is its mouth, with tentacles around the outside.

This brightly-coloured orange cup coral gets its colour from the algae inside it.

Grabbing food

The algae make energy in the daytime, when the sun is shining. At night, the coral polyps use their tentacles to grab passing prey to eat. Each tentacle is covered in tiny stinging cells called nematocysts that stun and kill the prey (corals are related to jellyfish, which also have stinging tentacles). The corals feed on food **particles** floating in the water, too.

Did you know?

Coral polyps are usually clear. It's the algae inside that give them their colours. There are several million algae inside each square centimetre of coral, which makes the colour look really strong and vivid.

When corals are born

On one or two nights of the year, an amazing event may occur on a coral reef, when the water above the coral fills with what looks like snow. It's called spawning and it's the moment corals are born. All the corals of one particular type release female eggs and male sperm into the water at the same time. An egg and a sperm join to create a free-floating planula – the name given to coral larvae. The planula will then find a home on the reef and turn into a polyp.

This coral is spawning – releasing eggs and sperm to make new coral.

The night that spawning occurs depends on the length of daylight and the temperature of the water. It usually happens several nights after a full moon. That's when the difference between high and low tide is at its smallest, making the waters calm enough for the eggs and sperm to mix.

Different ways of dividing

Some types of coral don't send their eggs into the water. Instead, the polyps keep their egg cells and gather sperm from the water. Then a little planula is born inside the polyp and leaves via the mouth to begin its new life.

Sometimes polyps divide themselves to make more polyps, instead of producing eggs or sperm.

Corals of the world

Stony corals

There are two different families of corals – stony (also called hard) and soft. The stony corals are the ones that build coral reefs. There are lots of different types. Some have pointed branches. Some are rounded, like boulders. In a location that has strong currents and churning waves, coral tends to grow in a more flattened spread-out shape that's less likely to get damaged. In calmer waters, more delicate branch-shapes can survive.

Staghorn coral is a common type of stony coral. It has round branches that can grow from just a few centimetres up to two metres long. It's found on Pacific and western Atlantic reefs.

a small staghorn coral

Pillar corals are among the largest of the stony corals. They can grow up to 2.5 metres tall. The reefs of the Caribbean and Florida are good pillar coral locations.

Table corals are an example of a stony coral that grows in a long, flat plate shape. It's not very colourful, but it makes a great shelter for little reef fish. The biggest one ever found grew off Indonesia and covered a whopping 53.5 square metres.

a pillar coral rising up from the seafloor

an example of a table coral

15

Named for the shape

Stony corals grow in all kinds of shapes, and often get their name from what they look like. For instance, the wiggly grooves over the surface of the rounded brain coral make it look like an animal brain. It can grow up to 1.8 metres high, and is found in tropical waters all over the world.

a brain coral off the coast of the Bahamas

The elkhorn coral gets its name because it's shaped like branching elk antlers. It can grow up to 3.7 metres wide. The Caribbean and the Gulf of Mexico are home to the most elkhorn.

a coral that looks like the antlers of an elk

Tube corals grow tube shapes that branch out in all directions.
They grow in different colours, including yellow, orange
and black. The best place to find them is in the southern Pacific.

You can see why tube
corals get their name.

Soft corals

Soft corals are bendable and they can sway in the current. They don't have stony outer skeletons. Instead, they have a strong inside core to support them. They don't have algae inside them like stony corals and they don't build coral reefs.

Gorgonian coral

This family of corals is found on coral reefs around the world. It includes long strands called sea whips, and sea fans that branch out like bushes. Gorgonian corals are often purple, red or yellow.

This diver has found some beautiful red gorgonian coral.

a spectacular pink carnation coral

Carnation coral

These particularly pretty corals look rather like flower blossoms
or mini trees. They grow in lots of different colours. They're
found mostly in the Indo-Pacific, in locations such as Fiji, Tonga
and the Great Barrier Reef.

19

More soft coral shapes

Soft corals tend to grow in spots below the stony corals on reefs.
You can often find them in sheltered locations under rocky
outcrops or in caverns.

Toadstool corals are a common example of a soft coral.
They look as if they have a stalk and a cap, just like a toadstool.
They can be pink, cream, brown or yellow, with white or gold
polyps, and they're common on many reefs.

Sea pens are soft corals that look like an old-fashioned quill pen
made from a feather. They can grow up to two metres tall and
they're brightly-coloured. They grow all over the world.

The toadstool coral is also called leather coral or mushroom leather coral.

an orange sea pen

Green bubble coral looks rather like a bunch of undersea grapes.

Bubble corals are soft corals with an unusual appearance. They look like inflated bubbles during the day but deflate at night when the coral's tentacles come out to grab food. Bubble coral is found in the Pacific and the Red Sea, and grows in different colours and sizes.

Corals that glow

Many corals have a surprising ability to glow in bright colours. This is called **fluorescence** and it helps protect them from dangerously strong sunlight. Cells inside the coral absorb the sunlight, alter it to make it safe and then **emit** parts of it as green and red light. As well as protecting the coral, the light show may also attract prey.

various fluorescent corals

More to learn

There's still lots to learn about how corals glow. It's thought that 70–90% of shallow water corals may do it day and night, though we can't always see the glow with the naked eye.

A different family of corals found in deep water emit really intense fluorescent light for different reasons, to help their algae make energy.

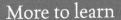

23

Life on a tropical reef

Coral reef creatures

The word "biodiversity" means
the variety of living creatures
found in a particular place.
Although coral reefs cover
less than 1% of the ocean
floor, they're amongst
the most biodiverse locations
on the whole planet.

a red sea cucumber off
the coast of Bali, Indonesia

Some animals live their whole lives on a reef.
Others visit to breed or to feed.
The two main **phylum** of reef
animals are the vertebrates
and invertebrates.

Many different animals can be
found on coral reefs, from tiny
fish to giant turtles.

Vertebrates are creatures with a backbone. Coral reef vertebrates include fish and sea turtles. Thousands of fish species – around a third of all marine fish types – spend at least some part of their life on a coral reef. Reefs make great nurseries where baby fish can get protection from pounding waves and hungry predators.

Invertebrates are creatures without a backbone. Coral reef invertebrates include brittle stars, tube worms, sea cucumbers, sponges, urchins and clams.
Corals themselves are invertebrates.

Did you know?

The most biodiverse coral reef region in the world is the Coral Triangle, the area where the Pacific Ocean meets the Indian Ocean around the equator. It includes Indonesia, the Philippines, Malaysia, Papua New Guinea and the Solomon Islands. It's home to a third of the world's reefs.

Who eats what?

A coral reef is the location for many food chains and food webs. A food chain is a simple pathway tracking who eats what in a line of connected creatures. Here's a very simple one:

marine plant	→	fish that eats plants	→	fish that hunts other fish

A food web is a network of all the food chains in one area. They can be broken down into trophic levels – which means levels made up of groups of animals that eat the same kind of food. Here are the trophic levels on a coral reef:

Herbivores – plant-eating animals. This includes microscopic free-floating creatures called **zooplankton**, which eat phytoplankton. These creatures are called consumers. They eat the producers.

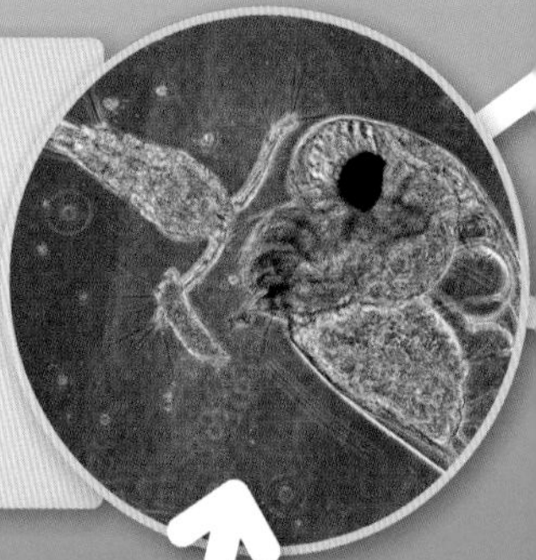

Marine plants – algae, seaweed and microscopic free-floating plants called **phytoplankton**. These creatures are called producers. They produce food using sunlight.

Carnivores that eat herbivores – meat-eating hunters such as some fish, lobsters and octopuses. These animals are called secondary consumers. They eat the consumers.

Carnivores that eat other carnivores – top predators such as sharks, rays and eels

Detrivores – they eat dead animals and waste material. This level includes brittle stars, sea cucumbers and shrimps.

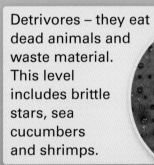

Omnivores – animals that eat both plants and other creatures. They include blennies, crabs and butterflyfish.

Decomposers – bacteria that break down dead material and return it as nutrients to the sea

Animals that work together

Some coral reef creatures rely on each other. This teamwork between different species is called symbiosis. Stony corals have symbiosis with the tiny algae that live inside them. The coral give the algae protection, and the algae give the coral food in the form of sugars.

Anemone and clownfish

Sea anemones grab passing fish to eat by shooting venomous threads from their tentacles, paralysing the fish. Yet clownfish live quite happily amongst the tentacles of an anemone, immune to its venom. The anemone gives the clownfish protection, and in return, the clownfish chases away butterflyfish that want to eat the anemone.

A clownfish nestles in amongst anemone tentacles, immune to the stings.

A pistol shrimp communicates with a goby by touching it with antennae.

Pistol shrimp and goby

Pistol shrimps and goby fish sometimes live in teams. The shrimp has bad eyesight but it's great at digging a burrow. The goby is bad at burrowing but has great eyesight. The goby acts as a guard for the shrimp, warning it with tail movements if there's danger. In return, the goby gets a safe place to live.

Cleaner wrasse

Cleaner wrasse set up "feeding stations" on reefs. The wrasse nibble small parasites and dead skin off visiting fish. That way the wrasse get fed and the fish get clean.

A cleaner wrasse cleans a surgeonfish.

Tropical reef animals

Reef fish shapes and colours

Small reef fish tend to have
a flattened body with fins
positioned differently to
an ordinary ocean fish.
This shape helps them to
make fast sudden turns, to
steer themselves around
the reef.

Coral reef fish that hunt others
by chasing them will
often have a very narrow
streamlined body, to help
them slip quickly through
the water.

The threadfin butterflyfish from
the Red Sea has a flat body and
fins positioned to help it make
fast turns. It cruises around
eating algae and zooplankton.

A needlefish in the Red Sea is shaped
to slip speedily through the water.

A stonefish is very hard to see on a coral reef.

Reef fish colour

Reef fish are often colourful and patterned. This helps them to recognise each other and find a mate. Sometimes, this acts as a warning that they're poisonous. For instance, the striped lionfish, which has venomous spikes, has very striking colours that act as a warning.

Some fish are camouflaged, so they can lurk unseen, waiting to gobble up passing prey. The stonefish is a good example of this. It blends into the seabed looking like stone, waiting to pounce. It has sharp venomous spines, and since it's hard for humans to spot, its stings are a common problem on the Great Barrier Reef.

Don't attack me!

Porcupinefish are found in most tropical reef seas. They're a good example of a reef fish that has a body shape designed to put off attackers. If it's threatened, the porcupinefish gulps in water to puff itself up, so it looks much bigger and its spines stick out.

The triangular trunkfish has its own armour to protect itself from predators. Its scales are hard plates and it has spines to deter its enemies. Many reef fish have body spines to keep predators away.

This porcupinefish is puffing itself up because it fears a threat.

A spotted trunkfish has armoured scales on its box-like body.

Mouths and teeth

Fish have different-shaped mouths and teeth, depending on what they eat. Predator fish need mouths that can swallow other creatures. Plant-eating fish need plenty of tiny teeth for cutting up plant material.

Parrotfish, found on reefs all over the world, are named for their beak-like mouth. They use it to tear off dead coral to get to algae. They munch up the coral with their sharp teeth, digest the algae and pass the coral out as sand in their waste. The beautiful white sand of Caribbean beaches comes mostly from the waste of parrotfish.

A parrotfish is using its beak-like mouth to nibble some dead coral.

Coral reef sharks

Sharks are the top predators on a coral reef. It's a good sign of a healthy reef if there are lots of them because it shows there's plenty of food for them to eat. They cruise around looking for a meal such as fish, octopus or squid.

Reef sharks

Reef sharks grow to between 1.6 and three metres long, but they don't usually attack humans. They can gather in schools of 100 sharks or more. Working together, they can trap schools of fish and then move in for an easy meal.

A Caribbean reef shark cruises a reef in the Bahamas.

Hammerhead sharks

Hammerhead sharks are very dangerous to humans. There are ten different types, and the biggest can grow up to six metres long. A hammerhead uses its strange-looking nose to sense prey hiding on the seabed. Electro-sensors on the nose can pick up tiny electrical pulses given out by living things.

a hammerhead shark in the Bahamas

Wobbegong sharks

The wobbegong shark gets its name from the Australian Aborigine words for "shaggy beard". It lurks on the seabed, hiding from enemies or waiting to grab passing prey. Flaps of skin around a wobbegong's nose help to hide it, along with its speckled markings. The biggest species, the spotted wobbegong, can grow up to 3.2 metres long and is found on the Great Barrier Reef.

a wobbegong on the Great Barrier Reef

Seahorses of the reef

Coral reefs provide a hiding place and a food larder for some types of seahorses. They wait for a meal to swim by, sucking up tiny shrimps and other mini creatures using a tube-shaped mouth. A seahorse has no stomach, which means that food passes through it really quickly and it has to eat almost all the time to get enough nutrients to survive.

Reef seahorses often have skin flaps that help to disguise them among the coral. The best example is the leafy seadragon, found off Australia. It has body parts that look like leafy branches.

Seahorses are getting much rarer. They're hunted and dried out to use in Asian medicine or sold as souvenirs, and this could lead to their extinction.

a leafy seadragon seahorse off southern Australia

36

Coral reef pipefish

Pipefish are related to seahorses. They have a long tube-like snout that gives them their name. They can hide in cracks and crevices on the reef, waiting to suck up a passing shrimp. Ghost pipefish – a related family – are true coral reef masters of disguise. They look just like seaweed as they lurk waiting for dinner.

an ornate ghost pipefish in the Indian Ocean

Crustaceans on the reef

Coral reef crustaceans are a family of marine animals that include shrimps, crabs and lobsters. They have a hard shell and claws.

Useful shrimps

Shrimps are a very important food source for other reef animals. The cleaner shrimp has found a way to avoid being eaten, however. It removes parasites from fish and other creatures, and in return, they don't eat it. Cleaner shrimps even clean inside the mouths of big hunters like grouper fish without getting swallowed.

A cleaner shrimp cleans inside the mouth of a moray eel and doesn't get eaten.

A Caribbean spiny lobster
patrols a coral reef at night.

Lobster visitors

Spiny lobsters are famous for their **migration** between shallow
reef-filled waters and deeper waters. They travel in a long line
on the seabed. When they arrive on a reef, they hide in crevices
during the day and wander around at night.

Cleaner crabs

Reef-dwelling crabs hunt living creatures, but they also
eat algae and dead animals, too, helping to keep the reef
clean and free from harmful bacteria.
Despite their protective shells, they're
hunted themselves. For instance,
an octopus can puncture a crab
shell with its beak.

An anemone crab is immune
to the stings of an anemone
living on a coral reef.

All about anemones

Coral reefs provide a home for many types of sea anemones. They attach themselves to a reef using a sticky body foot, and then wait to catch passing fish. Their tentacles are triggered by touch to fire out harpoon-like threads that inject a paralysing venom.

Most anemones have stings that are harmless to humans, but a few can cause great pain to divers. The Bali Fire anemone and the Hell's Fire anemone, found in the Indo-Pacific, both have a sting similar to a jellyfish.

Like coral, some tropical anemones are symbiotic with algae. The anemones provide a safe home for the algae, and in return, the algae provide food.

an anemone anchored by its sticky foot, waiting for its prey

Did you know?

A hermit crab will sometimes pick up a small anemone to put it on its shell. It might take the anemone with it when it moves shell later on. The anemone's tentacles help to protect it from predators, and in return, the anemone gets to eat titbits from the meals captured by the crab. The Pacific coral reef-dwelling boxer crab carries anemones in its claws, like pom-poms!

a boxer crab carrying two tiny anemones in its claws

Spiny reef-dwellers

There are lots of **echinoderms** on coral reefs around
the world. The word "echinoderm" means "spiny-skinned".
Echinoderms have an external skeleton made of hard plates, and
thousands of tiny tube legs to help them move around.

Sea urchins

Sea urchins eat plants and dead animal material. They're
round, with lots of protective spikes that they can swivel to
face predators. Some sea urchins have poisonous spines.

a colourful spiky sea urchin
off the coast of Indonesia

Starfish

Starfish – or sea stars – eat
small creatures and graze
on algae. There are many
different types, but they all
have five arms. If a starfish
loses an arm, it can grow
a new one.

There are over 2,000
different species of
starfish, and they're
found on all coral reefs.

Sea cucumbers

Sea cucumbers are filter feeders,
which means they collect tiny
food particles from the water around them. At one end of
the sea cucumber there's a mouth surrounded by tentacles.
If a sea cucumber is attacked, it has
an unusual defence. It turns
itself partly inside out,
pushing out its internal
organs to put off
the attacker! It then
grows new ones.

a large sea cucumber,
about 0.6 metres, off the coast
of a south Pacific island

43

Marine worms

Sea worms are very important on coral reefs around the world. Not only do they provide food for other animals, they help to clear away dead creatures and dead sea coral, too. Some types move around and others attach themselves to rocks.

a split-crown feather duster worm in the Caribbean

Feather duster worms have feathery tentacles that filter food particles out of the water. Tube worms hide inside protective tubes, while Christmas tree worms have lots of tentacles that look more like a plant.

Christmas tree worms on the Great Barrier Reef

Bristle worms wander around the sea floor collecting food. They're covered in tiny bristles to protect them. The sting from the bristles of a fire worm can cause a human pain and itching for weeks.

Flatworms look more like flattened pancakes than worms. They often have very bright colours, to warn enemies that they're bad to eat. The flatworm **excretes** a stinking gooey mucus if it feels threatened.

a gold dotted flatworm in the Red Sea

All sorts of molluscs

Molluscs include creatures with shells, such as clams and scallops. Sea slugs and nudibranches are in the family, too, though they don't have shells. Octopuses, squid and cuttlefish are also molluscs.

Gastropods

Marine snails called gastropods belong to the mollusc family. Some of these are plant-grazers. They use a tooth-lined tongue called a radula to scrape off the algae from reefs. Others are hunters. One group, the cone shells, can even inject lethal poison into creatures.

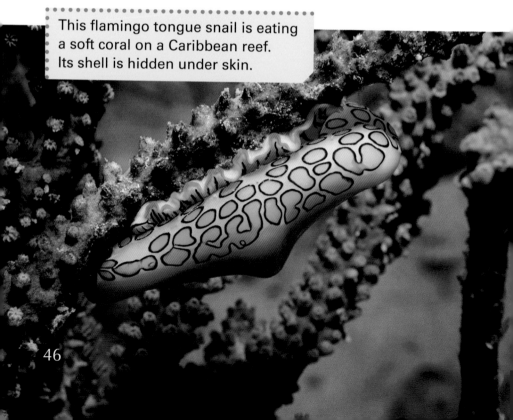

This flamingo tongue snail is eating a soft coral on a Caribbean reef. Its shell is hidden under skin.

gastropod shells washed
up on a Thai beach

To make a shell, a mollusc secretes a liquid from a part of its
body called the mantle. The liquid hardens into shell, and over
time, the mollusc will secrete more liquid to make its shell bigger.
It uses its shell to hide from its enemies.

Bivalves

A bivalve mollusc makes a shell in two halves. Clams, mussels
and scallops are examples. To feed, the bivalves filter food
particles out of the water around them. Their enemies must
find ways to break into their shells, either by drilling in or by
squeezing them open. Starfish can squeeze open bivalves with
their arms.

Special shells

The biggest molluscs with shells are the giant clams. They live on reefs in the Pacific and Indian Oceans. They grow up to 1.2 metres long or more, and they can live for over 100 years. They grow large because, like coral, they have a great hidden food supply provided by billions of algae that live inside them. They also filter out food from the water around them.

Giant clams are an endangered species. They've been overharvested by humans for their shells, and for body parts which are eaten as a delicacy.

a giant clam on the Great Barrier Reef

Did you know?

Pearls are made by oysters, clams and mussels when a grain of sand or a parasite gets stuck in the mantle – the body part that secretes liquid to make a shell. To prevent damage, the mollusc gradually coats the grain with nacre, the material it makes to line the inside of its shell. Mother-of-pearl is another name for nacre.

This oyster, from the Red Sea, contains a pink pearl.

The cleverest creatures

Octopuses, squid and cuttlefish are all types of a mollusc called a cephalopod. They're found on reefs around the world and they're amongst the cleverest reef creatures. They have large brains and eyes, tentacles for grabbing prey and a beak for chopping up food.

Did you know?
. . . .
Octopuses are clever enough to use objects as tools.
The Pacific coconut octopus carries its own coconut shells or clams around as armour!

A coconut octopus uses two clam shells to make a cosy hiding place.

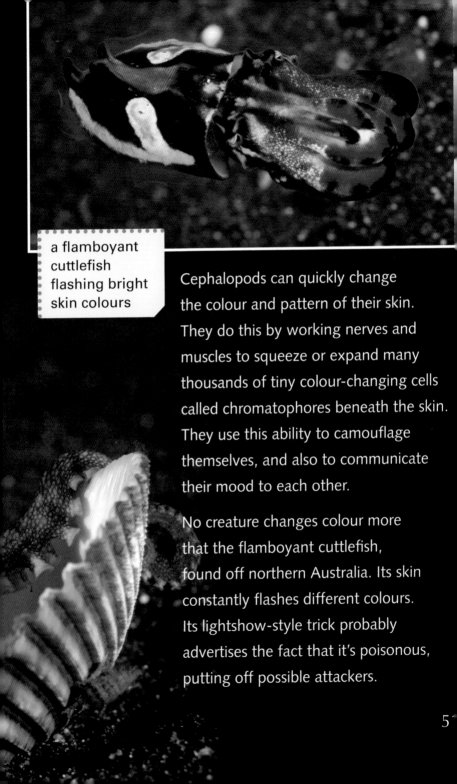

a flamboyant
cuttlefish
flashing bright
skin colours

Cephalopods can quickly change
the colour and pattern of their skin.
They do this by working nerves and
muscles to squeeze or expand many
thousands of tiny colour-changing cells
called chromatophores beneath the skin.
They use this ability to camouflage
themselves, and also to communicate
their mood to each other.

No creature changes colour more
that the flamboyant cuttlefish,
found off northern Australia. Its skin
constantly flashes different colours.
Its lightshow-style trick probably
advertises the fact that it's poisonous,
putting off possible attackers.

Watch out!

Some coral reef creatures sting humans. The geography cone shell can even kill people with its venom. There is no **antidote**. The victim must wait for the poison to wear off and hope to survive.

Geography cone shell

The geography cone shell lives in the Indo-Pacific. Because it's marked with brown and white patterns, divers sometimes decide to pick it up. To defend itself, the mollusc will stick a harpoon-like arm out of its shell and inject powerful venom.

a geography cone shell on the Indonesian seafloor

Fire coral

Fire coral is a type of
leafy-branched soft coral found
on reefs all over the world.
Its stinging touch feels like
burning, which is how it gets
its name.

fire coral in the Red Sea

Lionfish

The lionfish has venomous spines that can cause great pain.
It lives on the reefs of the Indo-Pacific, but now it's found in
the Caribbean and off the eastern coast of the USA, too. That's
because people bought lionfish for aquariums, found they grew
too big, and put them into the sea.

a lionfish with
venomous spines

Cold water coral reefs

Corals deep down

Corals aren't all warm water creatures. Some can live deep down in cold water, where there's little or no light. These cold water corals are only just becoming better known, thanks to **submersibles** and 3D ocean mapping. Cold water corals don't have any algae to provide them with food, so they don't need to live in sunlight. Instead, they grab passing food particles with their tentacles.

cold water coral growing off the coast of Norway

Cold water corals tend to live in spots where there's a strong current, bringing them plenty of food. They're found on **sea mounts** and on **continental shelves**. Like tropical corals, they provide a good home for other creatures, such as fish, starfish and sea worms.

Over 3,300 types of deep water coral have been discovered and named so far. There are probably lots more still to discover. They vary from single polyps the size of a rice grain to towering tree-like colonies up to ten metres tall.

Where in the world?

Cold water corals are found
in the Atlantic, the Pacific and
even off the coast of Antarctica.
They grow very slowly – no more
than 25 millimetres a year at most
– but over time they can form reefs.
A reef on Norway's Sula Ridge has
been growing for around 8,000 years.

The largest cold water reef yet found
is off the coast of Røst Island, Norway.
It measures 40 kilometres long and two
kilometres wide.

Going deep

To study deep water ecosystems, scientists
can send **ROVs** fitted with special
underwater cameras. In 1985, the wreck of
the *Titanic* was discovered 3.5 kilometres
down in the Atlantic, and ROV shots showed
deep water corals growing on it. It sank in
1912 after hitting an iceberg. Now it has
become an underwater ecosystem.

the bow of the *Titanic*, now home to cold water corals

Humans and coral reefs

Living by a coral reef

More than 450 million people live within 60 kilometres of a coral reef. Many of them earn money from reefs, eating and selling food gathered from the ocean and earning money from jobs connected to tourism. Countries benefit from having reefs, which bring money to the economy. But coral reefs are in great danger, threatening the lives of the creatures that live there and the livelihoods of many people.

A girl holds a sea cucumber caught on a reef off the coast of Malaysia. Sea cucumbers are boiled or fried and eaten.

a reef destroyed by dynamite fishing

Fishing the reefs

A healthy coral reef can provide lots of food for local people. Once, local communities used traditional fishing methods to harvest creatures from the reefs. Some local people still do this. For instance, on Pacific islands, fishermen sometimes use mini hand nets or woven baskets to catch their supper.

Modern fishing methods are much more of a threat to coral reefs. Some fishermen even use dynamite to kill fish, smashing up reefs in the process, or they may poison the water with cyanide, taking the large fish and leaving the rest to die.

Visiting a reef

Reefs are so beautiful that it's not surprising they attract lots of tourists to snorkel or scuba dive around them. Healthy reefs that are properly looked after make a lot of money. For instance, in Hawaii, reefs bring in over six million visitors a year and make over 11 billion dollars for the economy.

Diving is the best way to see the underwater beauty of a reef, but divers must be careful not to damage the coral. Once reefs are destroyed, the ocean wildlife around them disappears, so it's best to look, not touch.

a diver on a coral reef in the Red Sea

Dying reefs

Coral reefs are in serious danger around the world. Some scientists predict they could disappear altogether soon because of pollution, overfishing and climate change. If a reef dies, the creatures that live on it die, too. The people who live nearby lose food supplies and the money from visitors.

a patch of Pacific coral that has bleached

Corals are very sensitive to temperature changes in the water around them, to pollution and to careless damage. We can tell if stony corals start to die because they bleach, which means they go white.

When bleaching happen the corals push out the algae that live inside them and give them their colour. The corals lose the food supply provided by the algae. They may manage to survive and recover, but they're more likely to die.

Climate change

Many scientists believe that the Earth's atmosphere is heating up. It's called global warming, and it could be deadly to sensitive coral. A change of just one degree centrigrade in water temperature for one week will make coral bleach.

As the world's oceans warm, glaciers are melting fast in the far north and south of the planet. The added water is leading to a rise in sea levels. If stony corals find themselves in deeper water, with less sunlight, they die.

Climate change is leading to more ocean storms in some coral reef locations. Too many storms can damage reefs so much that the coral weakens and dies off.

Global warming and world pollution are increasing the amount of a gas called carbon dioxide in the air. The ocean acts like a sponge, absorbing the carbon dioxide, and the gas is gradually turning the water more acidic. Coral becomes much weaker and more easily damaged in acidic water.

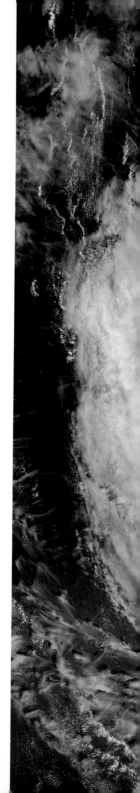

a satellite view of Hurricane Earl over the Bahamas in 2010. Global warming could bring more tropical hurricanes, meaning more wave damage to reefs.

Animal danger

Some creatures eat live coral, and it's thought they may help keep reefs healthy. But if too many of these creatures appear on a reef, the coral soon gets destroyed. This happens if there's overfishing. Creatures that nibble on coral grow in number if the fish that eat them disappear.

The crown-of-thorns sea starfish lives in the Pacific and feeds on live coral. In Australia, reef visitors are asked to report any sightings of crown-of-thorns, via a phone app or a website. That way, scientists can monitor the numbers and try to head off danger to the corals.

a crown-of-thorns sea star seen off the coast of Costa Rica

A blue triggerfish eats a sea urchin in the Red Sea. If the fish disappear, sea urchin numbers grow.

Overfishing can bring too many sea urchins and marine snails. Studies of reefs off the coast of Kenya have found spots where urchins are overgrazing on the coral and killing off sections of reef.

If too many algae-eating fish, such as parrotfish, are caught and taken off a reef, the algae can begin to grow too much, choking the coral and killing it. In the Caribbean, scientists are fighting to protect parrotfish, to help save reefs.

Human danger

Pollution kills coral. Chemicals and sewage that runs into the sea can kill coral. Fertilisers washed from farmland can make algae grow more strongly, choking the reef.

Soil particles called sediment can run into seawater when forests are cut down onshore, cleared for wood or for new building land. The particles can block out sunlight, helping to kill the coral.

Rubbish tipped into the ocean can kill coral reef creatures. Sea turtles can mistake plastic bags for jellyfish and eat them, blocking their stomachs so that they starve to death. Lost fishing nets can tangle up on reefs and trap creatures, too.

A sea turtle swims towards a plastic bag floating in the ocean. If it eats the bag, it'll die.

jewellery beads
made from coral

Coral reef mining is when corals are taken from underwater.
Sometimes whole sections of reef are removed to make bricks
or cement. Corals are also made into jewellery or souvenirs, or
sold to aquarium owners.

Saving coral reefs

A safe place for corals

Underwater coral reef nature reserves are being set up around the world. They're called Marine Protected Areas – MPAs for short. In an MPA, fishing and other industries are controlled to keep the reef undamaged. Local people and visitors are encouraged to help look after the reef.

Australia has created the world's biggest MPA network around its shores, covering a massive 3.1 million square kilometres. It includes the Coral Sea and the Great Barrier Reef. The reefs are monitored to make sure that they stay healthy.

a pontoon for divers on the Great Barrier Reef, now an MPA

MARINE RESERVE
TORTUGAS
ECO PARK
ISLANDS
TEAM
DISCOVERY
CENTER

a logo for Dry Tortugas National Park, a marine reserve set up off the coast of Tortuga in the Gulf of Mexico

Coral farming

Coral farming is a kind of underwater coral gardening. Small corals, the equivalent of plant seeds, are taken from a reef and grown in a tank. When they're large enough, they can be split up to make more corals.

Branching coral can be pruned rather like a bush, and the small pieces that are taken off can be grown separately. Corals grown this way in the right conditions can develop faster than corals in the ocean. Coral that has been ripped up by boat anchors can be saved, too, if the pieces are found quickly and taken to a nursery.

a tiny coral being grown in a coral farm tank

coral being grown underwater
off Tabawan Island, Malaysia

Corals that have been farmed can be replanted on a reef to
replace damaged areas. They can also be used in aquariums or
to make eco-friendly coral products.

Creating a coral reef

Man-made reefs can be created in areas of the ocean where the water is shallow and warm. Metal wire structures and even sunken ships can be seeded with coral from nurseries. If the coral grows, marine creatures will soon come to share the new living space.

The most successful man-made reefs are made from Biorock, invented by German scientist Professor Wolf Hilbertz. Biorock is made by a process called "mineral accretion".

A metal structure is anchored to the seabed and sends out an electric current, weak enough to be safe for fish and divers. The current causes minerals from the water to gather on the metal and gradually turn into hard material as tough as concrete.

Once the Biorock has grown, corals can be planted on it. They thrive on it because it's just like the limestone they'd make themselves. Biorock reefs have been created in over 20 countries in the Caribbean, the Indian Ocean and the Pacific.

Coral reefs are in great danger around the world. Hopefully, developments such as Biorock, MPAs and coral farming can help in the fight to preserve these incredibly rich underwater locations.

Biorock seeded with corals in the ocean off Indonesia

Glossary

antidote	a substance that stops poison from working; a cure
algae	a type of plant found in fresh or salt water
continental shelves	deep underwater shelves of land
echinoderms	a family of animals that includes sea urchins, sea stars (starfish) and sea cucumbers
ecosystem	a location where a big community of plants and animals live
emit	send out
equator	the imaginary line around the middle of the Earth
excretes	pushes out
fluorescence	sending out lightwaves that glow in bright colours
migration	yearly journey to another place
particles	tiny pieces of something
photosynthesise	make oxygen and energy (in the form of sugar) using sunlight, water and carbon dioxide
phylum	a group of animal families that all have something in common, such as a backbone (vertebrates) or no backbone (invertebrates)
phytoplankton	tiny plants that float in seawater
planula	tiny baby corals that float in the ocean until they find a home
ROVs	remotely-operated vehicles
sea mounts	deep underwater mountains
submersibles	small vehicles designed for going underwater
zooplankton	tiny animals that float in sea water

Index

Coral reefs of the world

North America

Gulf of
California

North
Atlantic Ocean

Europe

Gulf of Mexico

Africa

Panama

South America

South
Pacific Ocean

South
Atlantic Ocean

Arctic Ocea

Asia

Red Sea

Arabian Gulf

North
Pacific Ocean

**The Coral
Triangle**

Indian Ocean

**The Great
Barrier Reef**

Australasia

Antarctica

Ideas for reading
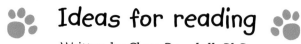

Written by Clare Dowdall, PhD
Lecturer and Primary Literacy Consultant

Reading objectives:
- make comparisons within and across books
- summarise the main ideas drawn from more than one paragraph, identifying key details that support the main ideas
- explain and discuss their understanding of what they have read, including through formal presentations and debates, maintaining a focus on the topic and using notes where necessary

Spoken language objectives:
- give well-structured descriptions, explanations and narratives for different purposes

Curriculum links: Geography – place knowledge; Science – living things and their habitats

Resources: Map of the world, key words on cards: *marine plants, herbivores, carnivores, omnivores, detrivores and decomposers,* ICT

Build a context for reading
- Look at the front cover, ask children what they see.
- Read the blurb together. Establish that a coral reef is a habitat found in some parts of some oceans. Share any ideas or experiences that children have about coral reefs.
- Ask children what they think coral and coral reefs are made from: plant, animal or mineral? Using what they know already, help them compile a list of questions to explore through reading.

Understand and apply reading strategies
- Read pp2–3 to the group. Using questioning, establish that a coral reef is an ecosystem made of minerals with animal and plant corals contributing to it, and living in and on it.